Contents

Words printed in *italic* are explained in the glossary.

What is nuclear power?

Nuclear power is a way of making electricity to provide light and heat for our homes, offices and schools. Nuclear power stations produce huge amounts of *energy*. But they also produce nuclear waste, which can harm people and our planet.

It takes a lot of energy to light up a city like New York.

Sellafield nuclear power station in the United Kingdom.

Why do we need nuclear power?

Most power stations make electricity by burning *fossil fuels*, such as coal or oil. But fossil fuels are running out, and they also give off harmful *gases*. So scientists have found other ways of making electricity, such as by nuclear power.

Understanding Pollution

Nuclear Waste

Lucy Poddington

First published in 2006 by
Franklin Watts
338 Euston Road
London NW1 3BH

Franklin Watts Australia
Hachette Children's Books
Level 17/207 Kent Street
Sydney NSW 2000

This book is based on *Our Planet in Peril: Nuclear Waste* by Kate Scarborough
© Franklin Watts 2002. It is produced for Franklin Watts by Painted Fish Ltd.
Designer: Rita Storey

Acknowledgements
The publishers would like to thank the following for permission to reproduce
photographs in this book.
Toshiyuki Aizawa/Reuters/Popperfoto: 28-29b; Klaus Andrews/Still Pictures: 5t, 20b;
Martin Bond/Environmental Images: 16tr, 17b; William Campbell/Still Pictures: 16tl, 17t;
Philip Carr/Environmental Images: 29t; Fred Dott/Still Pictures: 8tr; David Drain/Still
Pictures: 4bl; Mark Edwards/Still Pictures: 8b, 18-19t; Vasily Fedoseev/Reuters/Popperfoto:
16b; Dylan Garcia/Still Pictures: 23b; Herbert Giradet/Environmental Images: 9t; Pierre
Gleizes/Environmental Images: 12b, 18b; Pierre Gleizes/Still Pictures: 19t, 26b; Angela
Hampton/ Ecoscene: 6t; Paul Harrison/Still Pictures: 12-13t; Nick Hawkes/Ecoscene: 15b;
Hibbert/Ecoscene: 13b; Reinhard Janke/Still Pictures: 15t; Layne Kennedy/ Corbis: 27t;
Graham Kitching/Ecoscene: 4tr; Noel Matoff/Still Pictures: 26t; Juan Carlos Munoz/Still
Pictures: 25c; Jean-Francois Mutzig/Still Pictures: 21t; NASA/Still Pictures: 24t; Shehzad
Noorani/Still Pictures: 6b; Trevor Perry/ Environmental Images: 5b; Thomas Raupach/Still
Pictures: 19b, 29c; Roger Ressmeyer/Corbis: 25b; Mike Schroder/Still Pictures: 27b; Harmut
Schwarzbach/Still Pictures: 14c, 28-29t; Paul Seheult/Eye Ubiquitous: 13tr; Photo courtesy
of U.S. Department of Energy: 21b; Sabine Vielmo/Still Pictures: front cover; Adam Woolfit/
Corbis: 22t; Dave Wootton/Ecoscene: 7b.

A CIP catalogue record
for this book is available
from the British Library

ISBN 0 7946 6517 3
Dewey classification: 363.72'89

Printed in Dubai

People who work with nuclear waste must wear special suits that cover their whole bodies, otherwise they could become very ill and even die.

Problems with nuclear power

The waste that nuclear power stations produce is very dangerous because it gives off invisible rays called *radiation*. This can cause cancers in people and animals. It can also kill plants.

Dealing with nuclear waste

Nuclear waste can be buried or covered in concrete, but this does not make it completely safe. Scientists are trying to find better ways of dealing with it.

Power stations that burn fossil fuels give off harmful gases which pollute the air.

Fifty years from now

In fifty years' time, the world may use twice as much electricity as it does now. We need to work out how to make electricity without burning fossil fuels. We could use more nuclear power, but this will create more nuclear waste.

Using energy

Most kettles, cookers and fridges need electricity. How many other things in your home use electricity?

Every day, we use energy in many different ways. For example, we use energy whenever we switch on a light, turn on the heating or watch television. Energy is also needed to power cars, buses and trains.

Types of fuel

The main *fuel* used in the world is oil. In 1999, the world used 20,160 million litres of oil. Other fuels that are used include coal, natural gas and nuclear energy.

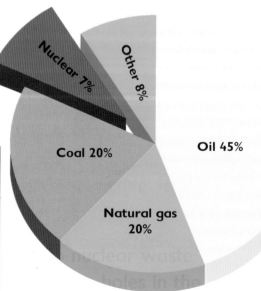

Nuclear 7%

Other 8%

Coal 20%

Oil 45%

Natural gas 20%

This pie chart shows the percentages of fuel used in the world in 2000.

In some countries, such as Bangladesh, many people do not have electricity in their homes. They cook food on fires.

How much energy do you use?

If your family has all the machines below, you will need a lot of energy to keep them working. Every year, you will use the energy that comes from burning 438 litres of oil.

Dishwasher
92 litres

Oven
84 litres

Fridge
128 litres

Washing machine
100 litres

Television
22 litres

Toaster
5 litres

Stereo
7 litres

◆ How you can help

You can help to reduce the world's energy problems by using less energy at home and at school. Turn off lights when you leave a room, and remember to switch off computers and TVs when you have finished using them. You can also save fuel if you walk or cycle instead of travelling by car.

The world's energy

People in Europe and the USA use much more energy than people in the rest of the world. In 1999, the USA used 25 per cent of all the energy used in the world. Even though China and India have larger populations, they used much less energy. However, more and more people in Asia and South America are using electricity, so in the future, the world will need to produce more energy.

In many countries, farmers use machines to harvest crops. The machines are powered by fossil fuels.

Fossil fuels

Fossil fuels, such as coal, oil and natural gas, are found in the ground. They formed millions of years ago from the bodies of dead animals and plants. We use these fuels in many different ways, but one day they will run out. They also give off harmful gases when they are burned.

Oil and coal

Oil provides the power for cars, trains and aeroplanes. The fuels petrol and diesel are kinds of oil. Coal is a black rock which is used in many power stations to make electricity.

Oil rigs are used to drill under the sea and bring oil to the surface.

This power station burns coal. Harmful gases pour out of the chimneys into the air.

Natural gas

Natural gas is a gas that burns easily. Scientists think that it gives off less *pollution* than oil and coal. Many new power stations use natural gas instead of coal.

Burning fossil fuels produces acid rain. These trees have been damaged by acid rain.

Harming the planet

Different gases are given off when coal and oil burn. One is carbon dioxide. This gas traps the Sun's heat in the *atmosphere* and keeps the planet warm. This is called the *greenhouse effect*. However, too much carbon dioxide in the air can cause *global warming*, which makes the atmosphere heat up too much. Other gases from fossil fuels can cause *acid rain*, which damages trees.

Fossil fuels running out

Experts think that there is enough coal to last for a few hundred years, but oil and natural gas will start running out this century. This is why we need to produce energy in other ways, such as nuclear power.

◆ **Science in action**

Make your own model of the greenhouse effect. Take two glass bowls and place a thermometer in each one. Put the bowls in the sunshine. Carefully place a piece of glass over one bowl. After one hour, measure the temperatures. Which bowl is hotter? The glass cover traps heat from the Sun inside the bowl. Gases in the Earth's atmosphere trap the Sun's heat in the same way.

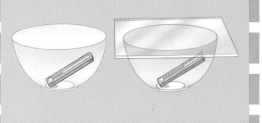

Nuclear energy

Everything in the world is made up of different types of *atom*. Atoms are tiny – for example, it would take millions of them to cover a full stop. Nuclear energy gets its name from the central part of an atom, the *nucleus*.

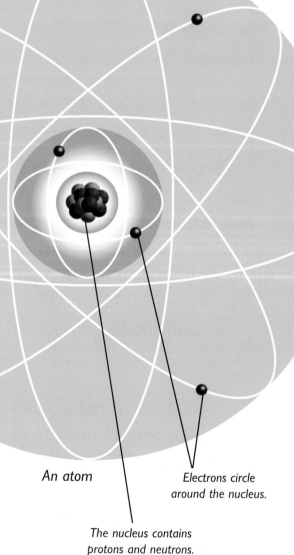

An atom

The nucleus contains protons and neutrons.

Electrons circle around the nucleus.

What is an atom?

Atoms are made up of smaller parts, called protons, neutrons and electrons. An atom's nucleus contains protons and neutrons. The electrons circle around the nucleus. In most *elements*, such as carbon, the atoms always stay the same. But in some elements, such as uranium, the atoms break apart and send out tiny pieces, called *particles*. These kinds of elements are called *radioactive* elements.

Radioactive elements

When atoms in a radioactive element break apart, they give off heat, light and radiation. The radiation can be particles, such as alpha and beta particles, or rays, such as gamma rays.

Alpha particles

The nucleus sends out some of its protons and neutrons. This radiation cannot travel through most solid objects.

alpha particle (protons and neutrons)

a new atom is formed

Beta particles

The nucleus sends out an electron. This radiation can travel through our bodies, but not through metal.

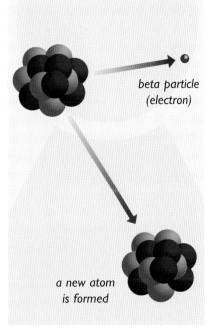

beta particle (electron)

a new atom is formed

Gamma rays

The nucleus sends out waves of energy. These waves can travel several kilometres, but cannot pass through lead or thick concrete.

gamma rays

Neutrons

Sometimes the nucleus sends out streams of neutrons. These travel further than gamma rays, but they cannot travel through water.

Staying radioactive

Radioactive elements take a long time to give off all their radiation. If an element takes 5000 years to lose the first half of its radiation, it will lose only half as much again in the next 5000 years, and so on. It will be a very long time before there is no radiation left at all.

Background radiation

Radiation is a kind of energy. It can be given off as light or sound, or as radioactive rays. Some kinds of radiation are all around us, such as radiation from the Earth or the Sun. This kind of radiation is called background radiation.

Radiation from the Sun

The Sun sends radiation to the Earth. The further away from Earth's surface you go, the more radiation there is. So, people travelling in an aeroplane receive more of the Sun's radiation than people on the ground.

Granite rocks such as these give off background radiation.

A lot of background radiation comes from the Sun.

Radiation from the Earth

Some rocks, such as granite, give off radiation into the soil and water around them. This is mostly harmless radiation, but sometimes rocks can give off the gas radon. Radon is very dangerous to people and animals.

Many homes have smoke detectors. These contain radioactive material.

Man-made radiation

If you have an X-ray, your body receives radiation. A small amount of radiation is also given off by smoke detectors. These types of radiation are not really harmful.

Geiger counters measure radiation.

Measuring radiation

A machine called a Geiger counter is used to measure how much radiation something gives off. It makes a clicking noise when it gets near radioactive material. The clicks get faster the more radiation there is.

Nuclear power stations

In a nuclear power station, the energy given off by atoms is used to make electricity. About 20 per cent of the electricity used in the world comes from nuclear power stations. In some countries, such as France, nuclear power provides around 75 per cent of the country's electricity.

Splitting atoms
Nuclear energy is made when an atom's nucleus splits apart. This process is called *nuclear fission*. The energy is turned into electricity for people's homes and offices.

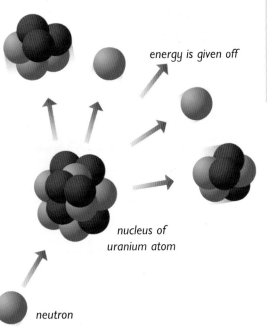

energy is given off

nucleus of uranium atom

neutron

A nuclear power station in Brokdorf, Germany.

Energy from uranium
Uranium is an element which is used as a fuel in nuclear power stations. Its atoms send out neutrons, which bump into other uranium atoms and cause nuclear fission. These atoms in turn make other atoms split apart, and so on. It is very important that the nuclear energy is given off safely, otherwise there could be a nuclear explosion.

How power stations work

In a nuclear power station, uranium is kept inside rods called fuel rods. There is a liquid around the rods which heats up when the energy is given off. This liquid then heats water to make steam. The power of the steam is used to make electricity.

Staying safe

The fuel rods are kept in a strong metal container for safety. The outside of a power station is made from concrete to stop radiation from escaping.

When the fuel rods have to be changed, the workers use machines to move them around.

Science in action

Put a small amount of sand into a test tube and use a thermometer to measure its temperature. Put your thumb over the end of the test tube and shake it hard for two minutes. Measure the temperature again. Moving the sand makes heat energy. This is what happens when an atom splits.

All workers are tested for radiation.

Power station workers

The people who work in a nuclear power station must make sure that they do not receive any radiation. They wear special clothes and stay away from the radioactive materials. They often do tests to check they have not been harmed.

How safe is it?

Like other power stations, nuclear power stations produce waste. Most of the waste from nuclear power stations is radioactive and very dangerous.

Some nuclear waste has to be kept in special barrels.

This sign shows that there is something radioactive behind the fence.

Never safe

All the fuels used in nuclear power stations carry on giving off radiation after they have been used. Some of them will never be safe.

Radiation sickness

If people receive a lot of radiation, their skin looks as though it has been burned. Radiation can also cause cancer.

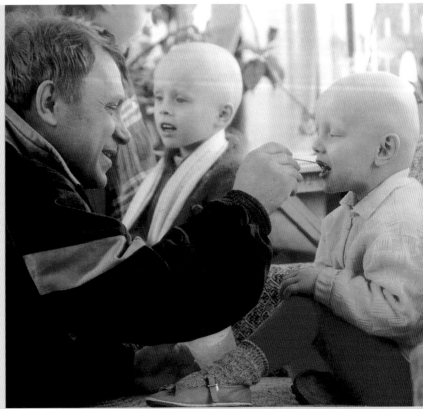
These sick children have received radiation from an explosion at a nuclear power station.

Streams and lakes can be polluted by radiation.

Living near a power station

People who live near nuclear power stations worry that they may be harmed by radiation. Radiation could come from the power station itself or from nuclear waste if it is not dealt with properly. People also worry that there might be an accident or explosion at the power station. The people who run the power station must keep checking carefully that no radiation has accidentally escaped.

Closing down

When a nuclear power station is not going to be used any more, it has to be closed down. However, the building will still contain radioactive waste, which needs to be made safe. To do this, the whole building is covered in thick layers of concrete to stop the radiation from escaping.

◆ Problem solving

Electricity can be made using the power of the Sun, wind or waves. Unlike nuclear power and fossil fuels, these kinds of energy do not produce any waste or pollution. We can use them as much as we want and they will never run out.

Solar panels use the Sun's energy to make electricity.

Dealing with waste

All the equipment used in a nuclear power station receives radiation and becomes dangerous. Even the workers' clothing needs to be handled very carefully.

Around the world

Many countries use nuclear power, but there are no agreements between countries on how to deal with nuclear waste. The next few pages explain what some countries do to keep safe, but other countries may not be as careful.

Some nuclear waste can be thrown away with ordinary rubbish.

Low-level waste

Some nuclear waste is not very dangerous, such as the clothing from scientists who work with radioactive materials. This is called low-level waste. It is usually taken away with ordinary rubbish and covered with a layer of soil. This is enough to block the radiation.

Dumping in the oceans

Some low-level waste is put in metal barrels and dropped into the sea. Britain stopped doing this in 1983.

Sometimes, barrels of nuclear waste are dumped in the sea.

Concrete stops nuclear waste from giving off radiation.

What is intermediate waste?

Intermediate waste is more radioactive than low-level waste. This means that it is more dangerous and must be dealt with much more carefully. Usually, this kind of waste is wrapped in steel and concrete. It may be kept near the power station it came from.

Burying waste

It is safest to bury intermediate waste in the ground. The waste will stay radioactive for hundreds of years, so the containers need to last for a very long time. The waste is put into steel drums and covered in concrete. Then it is buried in a pit with several more layers of concrete.

These barrels of nuclear waste have been covered in concrete and buried.

High-level waste

High-level waste is the most dangerous type of nuclear waste. It will stay harmful for over 100,000 years. Old fuel rods from nuclear power stations are high-level waste. Nuclear weapons that are no longer needed also produce high-level waste when they are taken apart. These kinds of weapons explode using the energy given off by atoms.

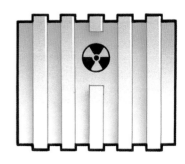

In one year, a nuclear power station produces an amount of high-level waste the size of a small car. Even this amount is extremely dangerous.

Used fuel rods from nuclear power stations are very high-level waste.

Water pools

One kind of radiation (neutron radiation) cannot travel through water. Some nuclear power stations wrap this type of waste in steel and concrete and keep it in pools of water to block the radiation. But this is not a good way to deal with the waste, as it cannot stay there forever.

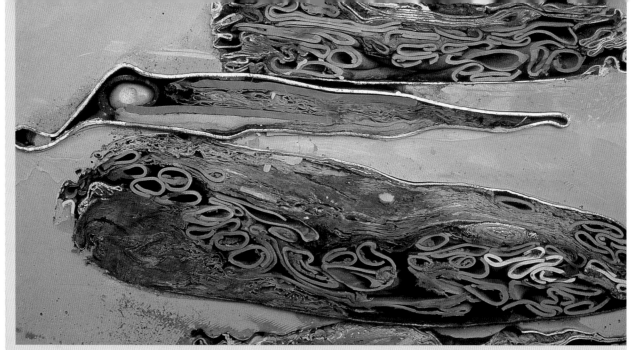
This nuclear waste has been covered in glass and cement to make it less dangerous.

Burying in glass

Scientists in some countries have decided to put nuclear waste in strong glass cases and bury them in deep mines. Glass is used because it does not rot or wear away.

Yucca Mountain mine.

◆ Science in action

Different things take different lengths of time to rot, or break down. Take two apples, two pieces of paper and two plastic bags, and place one of each on a window sill. Bury the rest of the objects in some soil. After a week, dig up the objects. Record what happened to them in the soil and on the window sill. Which object rots most easily? Which do you think might never rot?

Problems with mines

Scientists have to choose where to dig mines very carefully. If there was an earthquake or if a volcano erupted nearby, this could disturb the nuclear waste and let radiation escape. In the USA, a deep mine has been dug at Yucca Mountain, Nevada. Scientists are still trying to decide whether it is safe to bury nuclear waste here.

Solving the problems

So far, scientists have not found a safe way to deal with high-level nuclear waste. Teams of scientists are working hard to find answers to the problem.

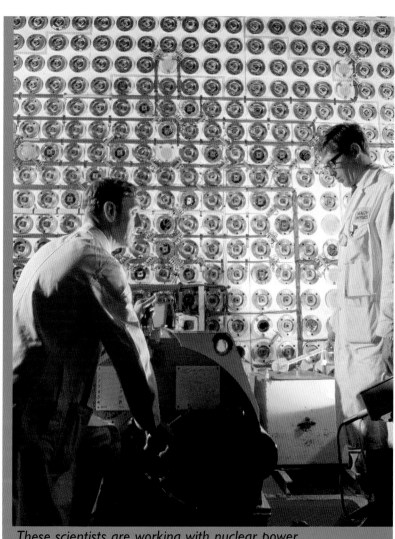
These scientists are working with nuclear power at Harwell in the United Kingdom.

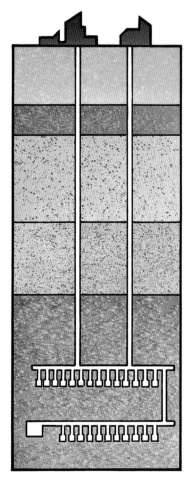
Nuclear waste could be poured into holes deep in the ground.

Possible answers

One idea is to heat up nuclear waste and pour it into very deep holes in the ground. The waste would be hot enough to melt the rock underground and mix in with it. Another idea is to drill holes in the seabed and pour the waste there. However, scientists do not know how safe these methods would be.

Using less nuclear fuel

Some nuclear power stations can make fuel last 50 times longer than usual. This means that there is less waste to deal with.

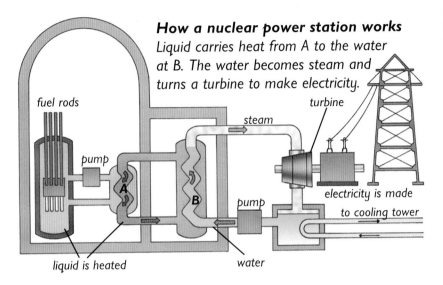

How a nuclear power station works
Liquid carries heat from A to the water at B. The water becomes steam and turns a turbine to make electricity.

fuel rods
pump
A
B
turbine
steam
pump
electricity is made
to cooling tower
liquid is heated
water

Making waste harmless

The best way to solve the problem would be to make nuclear waste harmless. If scientists could make it give off all its radiation quickly, it would stop being radioactive and would not be dangerous any more.

At Sellafield nuclear power station in the United Kingdom used fuel rods are changed into new ones.

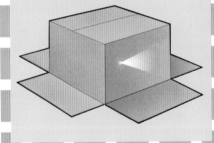
Reusing fuel

Once fuel rods have been used, they can be recycled to make new fuel rods. This means that old fuel rods do not need to be thrown away. It also means that less uranium has to be dug out of the ground to provide new fuel.

Nuclear fusion

Nuclear power stations use nuclear fission. They split atoms apart to create energy. But energy is also created when atoms join together. This is called *nuclear fusion*.

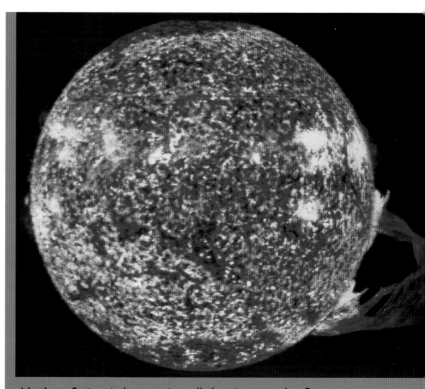

Nuclear fusion is happening all the time on the Sun.

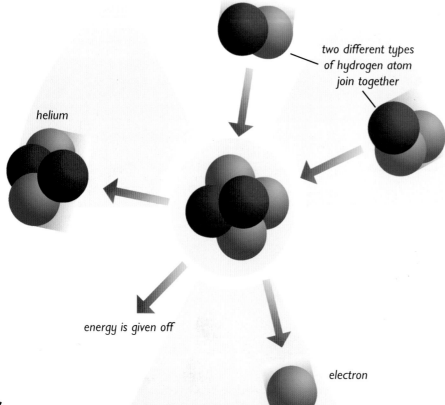

two different types of hydrogen atom join together

helium

energy is given off

electron

The Sun

The Sun's heat is made by nuclear fusion. The Sun is made mainly of a gas called hydrogen. Hydrogen atoms join together and make helium, another gas. When this happens, a lot of heat is given off. The temperature of the Sun is 10 million degrees Celsius!

24

Using nuclear fusion

Scientists are trying to make nuclear fusion happen in a laboratory. This could be a good way to make energy because we have plenty of hydrogen on Earth. Water is made up of hydrogen and oxygen.

No pollution

As radioactive materials are not used in nuclear fusion, there is no nuclear waste. This means that there would also be no danger of radioactive materials exploding.

Hydrogen for nuclear fusion could be taken from water in seas and lakes.

The problems

Many scientists think that one day they will solve the energy crisis and nuclear fusion will supply all the energy we need. However, for nuclear fusion to happen, there needs to be very high pressure and temperature. *Lasers* could be used to help create these conditions in a laboratory.

Scientists use lasers to study the stars. In future, lasers could help make nuclear fusion happen.

Points of view

Many people have strong views about whether or not nuclear power stations are a good idea. Organisations such as Greenpeace warn people about the dangers of nuclear waste. Many people are worried about whether nuclear waste will harm our health.

Greenpeace is an organisation which believes nuclear power stations are too dangerous.

This metal box contains used nuclear fuel. It is being unloaded from a ship in France.

Transporting waste

While nuclear waste is being moved from power stations to the places where it will be kept, it can give off dangerous radiation. Many people are concerned about this.

Nuclear protests

In 1997 in Germany, a group of protesters blocked a railway line because they wanted to stop nuclear waste from being transported. They disagreed with the government about where the waste should be kept.

Disagreements

In 1994 in the USA, nuclear power stations were allowed to store their waste on Prairie Island in Minnesota. It was agreed that the waste should soon be moved somewhere else. But the waste is still there because nowhere else can be found. The people who live on Prairie Island are angry that this has happened.

A room inside Prairie Island nuclear power station.

Government decisions

In some countries, the governments are concerned about the problems of nuclear power. For example, Germany's government has now decided to close down all of its nuclear power stations. In the USA, no new nuclear power stations have been built since 1978.

In Germany, people blocked a railway line where nuclear waste was being transported. The police sprayed them with water to try to make them move.

The future

Where will our energy come from in future? We will still need power stations to make electricity for our homes, offices and schools. But can energy be made without producing waste and pollution?

China has a very large population. It will need to produce more and more energy in years to come.

Fossil fuels versus nuclear

Most scientists agree that fossil fuels pollute the atmosphere and cause global warming. In 1997, government members from all over the world met in Kyoto, Japan, to discuss these problems. Many countries agreed to use less fossil fuel, but some countries, such as the USA, did not. Nuclear power does not give off any gases into the atmosphere, so some countries think that it is better than using fossil fuels.

In 1997, government members met in Kyoto to discuss global warming.

Fuel that never runs out

Unlike fossil fuels, the fuel for nuclear power stations will probably never run out. When nuclear fuel has been used, it is changed into new fuel that can be used again.

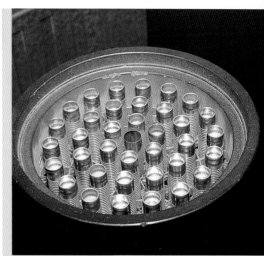
Nuclear fuel in these fuel rods can be used more than once.

Until scientists find out how to make nuclear waste safe, these barrels of waste will stay underground.

Making energy safely

Nuclear scientists are learning more about nuclear power. They hope they will find a way to make nuclear waste less harmful. They also hope that one day they will be able to create energy using nuclear fusion. This would be a huge step towards cutting down pollution.

Further information

There are websites where you can find out more about the topics in this book.

http://www.aecl.ca/ kidszone/ atomicenergy
Here you can learn about nuclear power and other ways of making energy.

http://www.eia.doe. gov/kids
On this website you will find energy facts, games and activities.

http://www.nei.org/ scienceclub
This website has interactive cartoons about nuclear power.

http://tiki.oneworld. net/penguin/energy/ energy.html
Find out all about energy with Tiki the Penguin.

http://www.bnfl.com
This is the website of British Nuclear Fuel. It has quizzes and games on energy, electricity and nuclear power.

http://www.wwf.org.uk/ gowild
This World Wildlife Fund website tells you about pollution and how you can help our planet.

http://www.greenpeace. org.uk
Here you can find out about Greenpeace, an organisation which aims to protect the environment.

Glossary

acid rain
Rain that is more acidic than usual.

atmosphere
A layer of gas (called air) wrapped around the Earth, like a blanket.

atom
A tiny unit of something, made up of protons, neutrons and electrons.

element
Something that is made up of only one type of atom.

energy
The power which makes people and machines move, or provides light and heat.

fossil fuels
Fuels made from the bodies of animals and plants that died millions of years ago.

fuel
Something that gives off heat and energy when it burns.

gas
A substance that is neither a liquid nor a solid. The air is a mixture of gases.

global warming
The warming up of the Earth's atmosphere, over many years. It is caused by gases in the Earth's atmosphere.

greenhouse effect
The way in which gases in the Earth's atmosphere trap heat from the Sun.

laser
A machine that sends out a very strong beam of light.

nuclear fission
When the nucleus of an atom is split apart. This gives off a lot of energy.

nuclear fusion
When two atoms join together, giving off energy.

nucleus
The central part of an atom.

particles
Very small pieces of something.

pollution
Dirt or harmful substances in the air, water or soil.

radiation
The energy that is given off when an atom splits into smaller parts.

radioactive
A radioactive material gives off radiation.

Index